GROWING UP
girl

Eileen McCrew

GROWING UP *girl*

Sharing your heart with your mom

EILEEN PETTYCREW

Saint Mary's Press
Winona, Minnesota

Genuine recycled paper with 10% post-consumer waste.
Printed with soy-based ink. 50455

The publishing team included Leif Kehrwald, development editor;
Roxanne Camron, copy editor; Barbara Bartelson, production editor;
Jeanne Icenogle, typesetter; Kelly N. Kofron, cover and title page designer;
manufacturing coordinated by the production services department of Saint
Mary's Press.

Printed in the United States of America

Printing: 9 8 7 6 5 4 3 2 1

Year: 2011 10 09 08 07 06 05 04 03

ISBN 088489-563-7

Library of Congress Cataloging-in-Publication Data

Pettycrew, Eileen.
    Growing up girl : sharing your heart with your mom / Eileen Pettycrew.
    p. cm.
ISBN 0-88489-563-7
    1. Daughters—Religious life. 2. Mothers and daughters—Religious
aspects—Christianity. 3. Pettycrew, Eileen. I. Title.
BV4860 .P48 2003
248.8'33--dc21
                                                                2002156102

For Annie Pettycrew
and Elena Jo Pettycrew

Author's Acknowledgments

I would like to express my deepest gratitude to the following people:

All the women who shared their stories with me, whether I was able to use them for this book or not. They opened their hearts and lives to me. It is an honor to have heard their stories.

Loretta Schaff, OSF, friend, mentor, companion on the journey, woman of God, whose ministry with women laid the groundwork for this book.

The mothers and daughters who graciously "field-tested" the sharing process that this book presents.

Leif Kehrwald, for his skilled guidance, gentle and helpful feedback, and unflagging confidence in my work.

Family and friends who offered encouragement and shared their enthusiasm for this project.

Jim Pettycrew, for believing in me.

Contents

Getting Started

One time when I was about five years old, I was eating lunch with my mom, my brother, and my sister. A big jar of mayonnaise sat on the table in front of me. For no apparent reason I picked up a spoon, stuck it in the jar, and plopped a glob of mayonnaise into my hair. Nobody noticed. I did it again and again, until I had a pile of mayonnaise on top of my head. I smeared it around like sudsy shampoo, letting the slimy goo squeeze out through my fingers. Finally my sister saw me. "Mommy!" she shouted. "Eileen put mayonnaise in her hair!" My mom took one look at me, let out a wail, grabbed my arm, and marched me to the sink for the first of many hair washings. My scalp was sore when she finished.

Why did I put mayonnaise in my hair? I have no idea. I just wanted to, that's all. Maybe I wanted attention. I got attention all right—a lot more than I bargained for! This story tells me something about me. This story lives in my heart.

How about you? What did you love to do when you were a little girl? What happy events come to mind? What outrageous things did you do? These experiences are *your* stories.

Now think of your life this very minute. Are you worried about next week's math test? Did your best friend start ignoring you today and whispering about you to the other girls? Is there a boy at your table who taunts you, telling you over and over how stupid you are? Are you nervous about your part in the school play? Are you excited and scared about singing a solo in the school chorus performance? These are also your stories.

All your stories live in your heart, in the place where you keep your secret thoughts and dreams. This is also the place where God lives inside you. As you grow, day by day, your stories collect in your heart.

Your life is like a spool of thread. From the instant you were born, your thread began to unwind from the spool, minute by minute, hour by hour, day by day, year by year, until it is where you are today. Your thread does not always unspool in a straight line. It might tangle, knot, twist, or coil. As your thread unwinds from the spool, your tangles, knots, twists, and coils—*your stories*—unfold and live on in your heart. Your stories become a part of who you are. They are the thread of you.

Believe it or not, your mother was a little girl once too. She was also a girl your age, growing into a woman. Your mom's thread still is continuously unwinding from *her* spool. She has her own tangles, knots, twists, and coils in her thread—her stories—that she has lived throughout her life. Your mother's stories continue to unfold moment by moment, just as your stories do.

It may be even harder for you to believe that your mother is still trying to grow up. She has not reached a magical age where she has all the mysteries of life figured out. There is no such age! She does not have all the answers. She makes mistakes. She gets confused. Like you, your mother has challenges and heartaches to face. She has times when she would rather not have to grow up. She has moments when she needs comfort, love, and courage.

What if you could talk with your mother and the two of you could share the stories that live in your hearts? What if you could meet your mother in a place where your hearts could come into view? What if you could peek into each other's world and learn about who the other really is? What if you could feel comforted, accepted, and understood, no matter what troubles you shared? What if by telling your stories you could discover how your thread intertwines with God?

Sparks in the Dark

Think about your bedroom when it's dark. Can you recall times when your mother tucked you in for the night, times when your room was so dark you could barely see her? What did that feel like? Did you feel safe, loved, and special? What if you were to invite your mother to share stories with you in the cozy safety of your dark bedroom?

Story sharing in the dark can be magical. As your mother tells a story, sparks appear. In the flash of light, you glimpse the girl your mother once was. You see that your mother had a real life that began many years before you were born. You understand that your mother may have gone through the kinds of difficulties and painful moments you are facing now. You discover you are not alone with your problems.

You begin to feel safe enough to share your own stories, trusting your mother to hear you with an open heart. Your stories send off their own sparks, and your mother catches a glimpse of the real you. You get the courage to tell her about the boy at school who taunts you. You confide your worry about next week's test. A problem you have held inside for weeks makes its way to the surface, and you tell your mom about it, knowing she will understand.

Does story sharing in the dark mean you tell your mother everything? It can. It can also mean that you will share with your mother only what you need to share. If that means keeping a few treasured secrets tucked away, secrets that you share only with the locked pages of your journal, that is your privilege.

Candle in the Corner

If you ever were a safety patrol guard at your school, you know that your job was to keep kids safe as they crossed the street. Wearing a neon-colored vest, holding out a large bright flag, you entered the crosswalk, signaling to oncoming cars that they needed to stop and let the children cross to safety. The children depended on you to keep them safe.

You and your mother need to feel safe to share what is in your hearts, as safe as little girls crossing the street under the sharp eye of the safety patrol guard. You both must feel protected from the oncoming cars of interruptions, misunderstandings, and judgments. On page 19 you will find "Guidelines for Safe and Secure Sharing." Abiding by these rules will help protect both you and your mom from negative interactions that could threaten your sense of safety and security.

"Quick Safety Guide," a summary of the safe and secure sharing guidelines, appears on page 20. You and your mom can use this guide for an easy review each time you gather to share sacred space. One way to do this is to light a candle together when your mom enters your room. Set the candle in a corner of your room, and, by its light, read the "Quick Safety Guide" aloud. This "reading of the rules" can become a part of your ritual together. Also, as you share your stories, the candle in the corner will remind you both that God is present.

How This Book Works

Each chapter focuses on a challenging part of growing up and is divided into the following sections:

Looking Back

This section presents a little girl's story and a young teen's story from the lives of real mothers.* Throughout the book, mothers look deep within their hearts to share tender, happy, and painful moments from their growing-up years. The stories show us that a mother's life takes root long before she becomes a mother, and she has a unique thread of her own, just as you do.

Finding the Thread

In this section we sift through the two stories to expose the thread of the real girl that lives through them. We search for signs of the little girl in the teen girl and in the woman she grew up to be. We ponder how the thread of the girl is inter-twined with God.

Talk Time

In "Talk Time" you invite your mother to join you in the dark-ness of your bedroom to share your own stories. Questions that relate to the particular topic of the chapter will help you and your mom get started with your story-sharing conversation.

Before you ask your mother to join you for "Talk Time," consider these ideas:

Find the best way for you to invite your mother to your bedroom. A fancy handmade invitation with an RSVP, an e-mail message written as poetry, a hand-delivered note on a plate of fruit, a phone call, or a face-to-face request are all ways you might try.

Ask for a time that fits into your schedules. About twenty or thirty minutes before your normal lights-out is a good time to start. Once you agree on a time to meet, do your best to honor your commitment to each other.

———————

* To protect the privacy of the mothers who share their stories in this book, I have changed their names.

Give this book to your mother and request that she read any chapter you have marked—the chapter that holds the most meaning for you this particular day.

Ask your mom to leave her "parent shoes" at the door when she comes to your room. Make it clear that your mom needs to step out of her role as a parent for a while in order to remember the girl she once was. If you think your mom might have a hard time taking off her parent shoes, ask her to bring along a doll or stuffed toy—her own from childhood or one of yours that she is fond of (with your permission, of course). Tell her you will have your favorite doll or stuffed toy with you too. Holding a doll while she talks may help your mom to slip more easily out of her role as your parent.

Candlelight Connection

After you have shared your stories, the candle in the corner takes on a bigger role. In "Candlelight Connection" you or your mother will carry the candle from its corner to a space between the two of you. As you sit across from each other, your faces glowing in the candlelight, you are invited to pray together, using the prayer written in the chapter or one of your own. After the prayer you can join hands and share a few minutes of silence. When you are ready, blow out the candle, share a hug with your mom, and go to sleep.

You and your mom may want to shop together for your candle. You could find one you both like and decorate it with wax cutouts that you make yourself or find at a craft store. The heat of your fingers softens the wax shapes so they stick to the candle. Or you may want to make your own candle from a candle-making kit. Of course, you may find a candle you like and buy it just the way it is.

This is a special time to share with your mom. Keeping your candle in your room and lighting it only when you share sacred space with your mom is a good way to honor your time together.

Sharing Summary

For easy review, a list of the steps involved in the sharing ritual appears on page 18. Refer to this summary whenever you need a quick refresher before you begin.

Practical Use of This Book

This book is for you to read and share with your mother. If you do not live with your mom, consider sharing the book during those times you are together. If your mom is no longer in your life, this book can be shared with the woman who is most like a mother to you.

Once you have read the introduction, encourage your mother to read it too so that she will have a general sense of the sacred sharing process. After she has read the introduction, your mother may want to invite you to a time of sharing. If she does, be open to her suggestion—just remember that you get to choose the chapter you want to talk about!

You can decide when you need to schedule "Talk Time" with your mother. Some days your thread will unspool in a straight line, and you will feel happy and content. Other days, your thread will knot or tangle, and you will feel sad, afraid, lonely, or angry. You will need comfort in your misery.

Depending on what is happening in your life, you may need daily or weekly conversations. Other times, a once- or twice-a-month "Talk Time" may be enough. It is up to you. Even if you do not have "Talk Time" with your mom every day, try to fit in "Candlelight Connection" as often as possible. It takes only a few minutes, and the reward is a closeness with God that you and your mom can share.

Other Ways to Use This Book

Although this book presents a way to share meaningful time and stories with your mother, you can use this book in any way that suits you best. Here are a few ideas for you to consider:

Together with your mother, light a candle in the darkness. Take turns reading the chapter of your choice. Share a time of silence with each other.

In the candlelit darkness, read the stories from the chapter you have chosen. Take turns sharing what you would have done if you were the girl in the stories.

After you read a chapter, write what you are feeling about it. Light a candle with your mother and ask her to read what you have written. Afterward, pray together or join hands and share the silence.

Gather some paper along with crayons, markers, or colored pencils. Light a candle together and read the stories aloud from the chapter you chose. Take a few moments to draw the image or picture that the stories stir in you. Ask your mother to make a drawing as well. Take turns talking about what you both have drawn. Or you might want to exchange your drawings without speaking, allowing the silence to be the gentle holder of your feelings.

Some Final Thoughts

This book is your invitation to talk, laugh, cry, and pray with your mother. It offers you a chance to get to know each other in a way you may not have thought possible. It is your window to yourself—the thread of you—and to your future as a woman. As you and your mother share your stories, it is my hope that you will enjoy many heart-to-heart conversations throughout your lives.

Peace and blessings as you grow into a life rich with possibility, fulfillment, and grace.

—*Eileen Pettycrew*
Portland, Oregon

Sharing Summary

1. Choose the chapter your heart is most drawn to. Read "Looking Back" and "Finding the Thread."
2. Read "Talk Time." Think about the stories you would like to share. Decide what questions you would like to ask your mom.
3. Ask your mom to read the chapter as well.
4. Choose a time for sharing.
5. Invite your mom to your bedroom.
6. Place a lighted candle in the corner. Turn off the lights.
7. Review the "Quick Safety Guide."
8. "Talk Time":
   Share your stories.
9. "Candlelight Connection":
   Place the candle between you and your mom.
   Say the prayer together.
   Sit in silence for a few minutes.
   Blow out the candle.
   Share a hug with your mom and go to sleep.

Guidelines for Safe and Secure Sharing

When you come together in the darkness, prepare your heart to listen. Imagine that your heart is opening up like a poppy, ready to drink in the warming rays of the sun.

Let the other person express her feelings without fear of being shut down. Feelings are neither good nor bad; they just are. Even if you do not understand how the other person can feel a certain way about something, accept her feelings as a part of who she is. It does not help to respond, "You shouldn't feel that way," no matter how well-meaning the comment.

Wait until the other person is finished sharing before speaking. Avoid interrupting to state your opinion or interject your own experience.

Get in the habit of offering a kind gesture—a gentle squeeze of the hand or a soft pat on the shoulder—when the other is finished sharing.

Give yourself time to respond after you have heard a story. Saying nothing is often the best response when you do not know what to say. Let the silence settle between you like a soft blanket, knowing that God is present within it. Trust that any words you need to say will come to you at the right moment.

When it's your turn to talk, give yourself permission to reveal only what you feel right about sharing. Check in with your heart before you speak, and trust what your heart tells you.

Give each other the freedom to share with complete confidence. You may want to make an agreement that certain things you reveal during "Talk Time" will not be shared outside of the room.

Above all, enjoy each other as God enjoys you. You are precious in God's eyes.

Quick Safety Guide

1. Prepare your heart to listen.
2. Accept the other person's feelings without judgment.
3. Wait until the other person is finished sharing before speaking.
4. Offer a kind gesture when the other person is finished sharing.
5. Give yourself time to respond after you have heard a story.
6. Reveal only what you feel right about sharing.
7. Allow each other to share in complete confidence.
8. Enjoy each other as God enjoys you.

Chapter 1 *tangles*
When Your Body Changes

Looking Back

These stories come from my childhood years in California.

A Little Girl's Story

I climbed on the bus and found a seat close to the front. I smoothed my pink gingham dress and crossed my ankles, settling in for the ride to kindergarten. Uh-oh, I thought. It's Friday and I forgot to wear long pants.

Friday was tumbling day, and Mrs. Hultz said girls could tumble on the mats as long as we remembered to wear pants. I loved Fridays. It meant I could stand on my head, something I could do better than anybody in the class. I shrugged. Oh, well! I wasn't about to let a little detail like forgetting to wear pants keep me from performing my favorite trick in front of everybody.

When I got to school there was a visitor in the classroom. Mrs. Hultz introduced her and said our visitor would be staying with us for the entire morning. I shivered with excitement.

This was even better! I couldn't wait to show our visitor how I could stand on my head. Wouldn't she be surprised! I watched the clock all morning. The minutes passed by so slowly. At rest time I wiggled and tossed on my pink rug, while eyeing the other kids lying still on their rugs. How could they do that? It felt as if there were jumping beans in my stomach that were keeping me in constant motion. All I could think about was convincing Mrs. Hultz to let me do a headstand, especially today of all days when I had a visitor to show off for.

At last Mrs. Hultz signaled two boys to push the chairs and tables back and roll out the mat. I tried hard not to squirm as I sat with the other kids on the floor. Mrs. Hultz stood at one corner of the mat with our visitor. I knew what I had to do.

I skipped to Mrs. Hultz. "Can I please do a headstand, Mrs. Hultz? Please?" I pleaded. I just had to stand on my head today. I just had to. I wanted her to understand how important it was to me.

I could see Mrs. Hultz's eyes soften behind her glasses. "Well . . . ," she began. I was afraid to move. Would she say yes? Mrs. Hultz glanced at our visitor and back to me. I could see she was thinking about it. "Well . . . okay," she said. I could tell she wasn't sure it was a good idea, but she had said yes. Thrilled, I bounced away before she could change her mind.

I made my way to the center of the mat. The room was suddenly quiet. I took my time, eating up each delicious second that I had everyone's attention. I placed my hands on the mat, planted my head in just the right spot, and whoompf! I kicked up my legs and held them together, straight as arrows over my head. The skirt of my dress puddled around my head, forming a perfect pink tent. I knew my underwear was showing, but I didn't care.

Nobody said a word. Seconds ticked by, then minutes. I was determined to stay up as long as I could to really impress our visitor. My head began to pound as blood rushed to it and my pink tent heated up. Now I imagined my dress was a hot air balloon, carrying me above the clouds. Through the pink I heard whispers from my classmates.

"It's time to get down now, Eileen," Mrs. Hultz called out.

What? She wants me to stop? I just got started! I pretended I didn't hear her.

"Get down now," repeated Mrs. Hultz, louder this time.

I straightened my legs even more and pointed my toes to the ceiling. How could she ask me to get down now? My magnificent pink balloon carried me even higher. The whispers turned into giggles and shouts.

"Eileen, get down!" boomed Mrs. Hultz.

I could have stayed up forever, but I didn't want Mrs. Hultz to be angry with me. I put down one leg, then the other, flipped up my dizzy head, and shook it. With a whoosh of hot air, my soaring pink balloon collapsed. A sea of faces swam into view. Catching the eye of our visitor, I flashed her a big grin. I was so proud of myself.

A Young Teen's Story

I loved to sing in the school choir. I especially loved choir practice during Advent—the Christmas carols were my favorites. Sister taught us beautiful harmonies that transformed us into a heavenly host of angelic voices.

In my seventh-grade year, I noticed a disturbing change. As I poured my heart into my singing, sweat would pour from my underarms and soak my school blouse and sweater. After every choir practice, I returned to the classroom with wet, uncomfortable underarms. Even more disturbing was the odor I noticed. Could others smell it too? Though I convinced myself that they couldn't, I became self-conscious about raising my hand in class.

Every morning before choir practice I told myself I would not sing my heart out. I promised myself to take it easy and not get carried away. However, as soon as I found my place in the choir loft, as soon as Sister raised her arms to direct us, as soon as my aunt played the first notes on the organ, I was lifted into the clouds. I sang with my whole heart, my whole soul, my whole being, and my sweat glands belted out their own accompaniment. Singing with half a heart was impossible, so I decided I would live with my soggy underarms.

One afternoon in class, after an especially rousing morning in choir practice, Sister read to us from Charles Dickens's *A Christmas Carol.* If Christmas carols had the top spot on my list of favorite things, the story of Scrooge was a close second. Inside the warm and cozy classroom, protected from the cold gray afternoon, I sat at my desk in the front row, savoring the story Sister read with such expression.

Sister paused to ask the class a question. Hands shot up, including mine. Sister called on David, who sat across the row from me. David stood up to answer, and to my horror I saw he was holding his nose. I knew what he smelled was me! My face burned with a flush that crept up from my toes. I caught a glimpse of Sister. Her mouth twitched, and I knew she was trying hard not to smile.

I wished I could disappear into the pages of my Scrooge book. David was just plain rude. I wanted to pull out his frizzy brown hair by the roots. How could he be so nervy? I was mad at Sister too. How could she think it was funny? How could she even think of smiling when I was so humiliated?

There was no way I could tell my mother when I got home. I was too embarrassed. Certainly no one else in the world had a problem like mine. I felt like a freak. The worst part of it was that choir practice would never be the same for me. How could

I sing like I wanted to sing if I had to worry about stinking up the whole classroom?

That night I searched for a sweater that did not smell. I couldn't find one. In despair I threw myself on the bed and cried. For the next few days I hid my heart during choir practice and sang with a weak, lifeless voice. I kept my arms clamped to my sides in class, fearing that someone else would notice the odor.

Finally, my mother noticed my problem and bought me a powerful deodorant. After using it awhile, I again found the courage to sing with my whole heart, my whole soul, and my whole being. I raised my hand in class without worrying and got over being angry with Sister. My anger with my body for changing and causing me so much grief, though, took a little longer to disappear.

Finding the Thread

Has there ever been a time in your life when everything was going along great and then suddenly everything began to go wrong? That happened to me as a young teen when I developed my odor problem. I suffered intense humiliation and felt betrayed by my own body. Not only that, I felt deprived of one of my greatest pleasures: singing with every part of my being. I became sick at heart. My life, my thread, had become massively tangled.

Things were much different when I was a kindergartner. Then I was determined to let nothing keep me from what I loved to do. I was not embarrassed about showing my underwear to my teacher, the visitor, and the class on the tumbling mat that Friday. My only regret was that I did not get to stand on my head as long as I wanted!

When I was a young teen I still knew what I loved to do, but the confusion, the tangle, caused by my changing body kept me from doing it. I felt I had to hide my heart so others would not discover my secret problem. Until my mother noticed and gave me the help I needed, I kept my little-girl heart tucked away beneath the tangle. Only then, slowly, was I able to let my heart out once again and burst into joyous song. Step-by-step along my thread, God was there, delighting in my exuberance, crying in my despair, and rejoicing when I sang with my whole being.

God lives in my heart and embraces the little girl and the young teen I once was. Today I still know what I love to do, and I know God loves me no matter how tangled the threads of my life become.

Talk Time

What tangles are in your thread right now? Is your body changing? Are you noticing body odors that were never there before? Are you worried others are noticing them too? Is your hair oily no matter how often you wash it? Is your face breaking out? Is your changing body making you feel unhappy and confused? Perhaps you feel as I did at your age and you are mad at your body because it is keeping you from doing the things you love.

Now think of a time as a little girl when you did something with your body that you were especially proud of. Maybe it was a time you danced or sang with every ounce of yourself. Sit with the memory for a few minutes. How does your little-girl heart show itself in your life today? Where is the thread of you?

As you and your mother settle in your room, ask her to tell you about when she was a girl your age. What sort of things happened to her? When did her body begin to change? Did anything embarrass her? How did she cope? What kind of help did she get? What story can she share about a time she poured everything she had into something she loved? How does she know her little-girl heart is alive and well today?

Candlelight Connection

When you and your mom have shared your stories, bring the candle in the corner to a space between you. Take a few moments to enjoy the warm glow of the candle, basking in the light of God. Say this prayer together:

My tangles are a part of me, God.
They make me who I am.
But sometimes I get embarrassed,
And I want to hide my heart away.
I don't want my body to change.
I don't want my thread to tangle.
But it does, God, and that's where you come in.
You love me, tangles and all.
You show me tangles can be beautiful.
You give me courage to let my heart out again.
You use my tangles to make me into a new creation,
Growing closer to you every day.

Now join hands and sit in silence for a few minutes. Let the silence speak across the candlelight. Feel God in your heart, intertwining with the thread of you, tangles and all. Feel the love of God flowing through your fingertips as you hold your mom's hands. Feel God surrounding you and your mom with a tent of radiant love.

When you are ready, blow out the candle, share a hug with your mom, and go to sleep.

Chapter 2 # knots

When Worry Strikes

Looking Back

These stories come from Elizabeth, a mother who grew up in Oregon.

A Little Girl's Story

From the time I was four years old, I spent a lot of time in a ravine that wound down to a natural creek. The ravine stretched from our backyard to the length of at least two city blocks and was surrounded by steep, tree-covered hills. The trees were so dense they hid the houses on the hills, giving me the feeling that I was all alone in a forest.

No established trails existed through the ravine, so I always blazed my own path to the creek. The ravine was full of what we called "sticker bushes." I was forever getting my clothes caught on them, but snags on my clothes did not stop me from spending every minute I could in the ravine. I wrote messages in the dirt, built forts, and gathered twigs and leaves for magic potions. At the creek I constructed miniature houses with stones, built dams with sticks, or floated leaves in the water to see where the current would carry them.

One day I was playing around in the ravine when I spotted something jutting out from the muddy ground. I poked at it with my walking stick and saw that it was the dark-green metal edge of something. Excitement surged through me. Could it be a box of buried treasure? a forgotten stash of cash that someone had hidden? a top-secret letter that would shed light on an unsolved mystery?

Using a walking stick as a tool, I dug around the edges of the metal until I had carved a deep trench around the box. I tossed the stick aside, plunged my hands into the ditch, grabbed the edges of the box, and yanked it from the ground. With shaking hands I lifted the latch on the box and opened the lid. Money! I grabbed the bills and spread them in my hands. Three one-dollar bills! My discovery wasn't exactly a pirate's treasure of gold coins, but I was thrilled. Here was one more reason to spend every minute I could in the ravine.

When I was five or six, I had a dream about the ravine. In the dream I was asleep in my bed when I heard breaking glass and the shuffle of shoes on the floor. I scrambled out of bed and sneaked into the hallway. Peeking around the corner into the dining room, I saw two men dressed in dark clothing with black scarves over their faces. They pointed flashlights here and there, obviously looking for something. A chill went down my spine; I feared they wanted to kill me. I had to escape. When their backs were turned, I streaked past them and bolted out the back door. I made it to the ravine in seconds flat. Huffing and puffing, I crouched behind a shrub and waited. The men never found me. I was safe.

I had variations of the same dream for many years. In fact, I still have this dream sometimes. The dream has never frightened me. I have always known I could escape to the safety of the ravine.

A Young Teen's Story

I was the ugliest girl in the sixth grade. I had a small head combined with big eyes, a big nose, a big mouth, and big freckles, topped off by big frizzy hair. In a classroom full of girls with little features and normal-sized heads, I felt I resembled an alien. My looks didn't improve over the next two years. In seventh grade I used lemon juice to bleach my big brown freckles. In eighth grade I wore gobs of blue eye shadow, which only made me look like a clown. The popular girls laughed in my face, not even bothering to whisper their scathing comments behind my back.

I bounced between fretting that I would be ugly forever and believing that one day I would be magically transformed into a beautiful girl with straight blond hair, a ski-jump nose, and a peaches-and-cream complexion. If only I wished upon the right star, closed my eyes in a tunnel and raised my feet, or blew out all my birthday candles at once, my wish would be granted and I would be beautiful.

When my oldest sister went to college, she left behind a collection of teen books. One of the books included a story about an ugly girl who wished upon a falling star one night and wound up the belle of the ball. I read this story twenty or thirty times. In the story the girl looks in the mirror the morning after the ball and is astonished that she has not changed at all. Because she believed that her wish on a falling star had come true, she had acted as if she were beautiful, and the boys at the dance had believed it too.

Baloney! This believing-she-was-beautiful business sounded suspicious to me. I was convinced the falling star had been responsible for the happy ending, and I was determined to concoct my own happy ending. Many nights I went to bed wishing I would wake up pretty, only to be disappointed when I faced my reflection in the morning.

Despite my fixation on my looks, there were times I could forget that I was ugly. I ate heartily, laughed with my friends, and rode my bike around the neighborhood. Then out of nowhere, some cruel kid would remind me of my flaws. Miss Lane, our seventh-grade teacher, often paired us up for projects. One day she lined us up at the back of the classroom and made her assignments. Pointing at Patrick, she directed him to work with me. Patrick made a face and blurted, "Ewww! Not her! She's ugly!" Gales of laughter filled the classroom while I stood red-faced among the more acceptable looking girls. As usual Miss Lane ignored the boy's outburst, which hung in the air like underwear on a clothesline, flapping in the breeze.

In the evenings I watched my favorite sitcoms on television, all of which showed teenagers dating and going to dances. Based on how teen life was depicted on television, I believed that girls needed a date to attend a high school dance. Because I seemed doomed to be forever hideous, I began to worry. What boy would ever ask me to a high school dance? Everybody would notice that I wasn't at the dance. Everybody would know I couldn't get a date. I couldn't imagine a more humiliating scenario. High school became something I dreaded.

First, though, I had to get through the seventh- and eighth-grade dances. These were held during the school day, so there was no getting out of them. One afternoon Miss Lane led us into the cafeteria, where the boys bunched into one corner, the girls in the other. When Miss Lane gave the signal, the boys rushed over to nab the cutest girls for the first dance, leaving us rejects to wallow in embarrassment. "Now boys," said

Miss Lane when the first song ended, "pick a girl who hasn't danced yet."

Wishing I could recede into the corner, I waited long, excruciating minutes while the boys slithered like snails to our side. One of the boys who had made fun of me in class approached and mumbled, "Wanna dance?" I nodded, and off we went. One look at his face told me he'd rather eat a plate of brussels sprouts than be my dance partner.

After the dance worry nagged at me like a hungry puppy. Convinced that no boy would ever ask me to a high school dance, I hatched a plot to save myself from the humiliation of not having a date: Right before the first dance, I would pay a doctor to put a cast on my leg. I figured that if my leg were in a cast, everyone would assume I had missed the dance because I had broken my leg, not because I couldn't get a date. My excuse would be visible for all to see. To pay for the cast, I saved all of my baby-sitting money and stashed it in a wooden box under my bed. For over a year every dollar I earned went into the box.

I began high school with a large chunk of money saved and a fierce determination to seek out a sympathetic doctor who would put a cast on my leg. As the first dance of the school year approached, my anxiety mounted. Would I be able to pull off my plan? What if the doctor refused to put a cast on my leg? What would I do?

One day at school I overheard a cluster of girls talking about the dance. No one mentioned dates. They discussed going to the dance as a group! Relieved beyond belief, I made plans with my childhood chums to attend the dance together. At the dance we stood in a clump, carrying on urgent conversations as if we hadn't talked all afternoon about what we would wear that night. No one asked me to dance, but no one asked my friends either, so I didn't care. All my worry had been for nothing.

At the end of my freshman year, I got a surprise: During a play rehearsal at the local theater, a heavy prop fell on my right foot and broke it. I ended up in a cast after all! Over the summer I got another surprise: Although I didn't wake up magically transformed into a beautiful blond, I grew into my features and blossomed into my own version of beauty.

Finding the Thread

Have you ever been worried about something? Have you tossed and turned at night, consumed with worry, unable to sleep? Or was it the kind of anxiety that constantly gnawed at you, eating away at your peace of mind? When Elizabeth was a young child, she found—right in her backyard—a place she could call her own, a place she could spend hours digging for treasure, building, playing, being alone, and being herself. The ravine was her source of peace and freedom. Later the ravine showed up in a recurrent dream as an escape route from dangerous men she feared would kill her. In her dream the ravine symbolized a refuge from all danger.

During her young teen years, worry slipped into Elizabeth's heart and left no room for the peace she had experienced as a little girl playing in the ravine. Based on her classmates' rude assessments of her looks, Elizabeth fretted constantly that boys would shun her in high school. Her thread filled with knots as she worried that everyone would notice her absence at the dances and think she could not get a date. Afraid that she would never be beautiful, and continuing to worry that she would be forever dateless, Elizabeth cooked up an outlandish scheme that she hoped would shield her from future humiliation.

The future Elizabeth feared never happened. Not everyone took dates to the high school dances. She attended the first dance with friends, and it did not matter to her if no one asked her to dance: No one asked her friends, either. All of her worry had been for nothing. She discovered that she needed only to let go of her anxiety and allow herself to let God take over. She needed only to look to her dream of the ravine to realize that the physical refuge of her little-girl years had been transformed into a peaceful inner landscape—a place she could enter at any time.

Elizabeth got a big surprise when she actually did end up with a cast on her leg. Here was life staring her in the face, nudging her to exchange worry for greater faith in a God who offers the gift of perfect peace. The happy ending she craved—that she would wake up beautiful—did not happen as she had hoped. True to form, God had another plan in store for her: In time she grew into her own unique beauty. Today she is a woman of vision and vitality who opens her heart to the ever-present love, joy, and peace of God.

Talk Time

What are you worried about right now? an upcoming test or school presentation? boys? friends? clothes? your looks? a soccer game or swim meet? a school dance? your parents? Maybe you are unable to pinpoint your anxiety to anything in particular. Is your anxiety causing you to lose sleep? Is your heart so filled with worry knots that there's no room for anything else?

Close your eyes and think about a time as a little girl when you were completely at peace. Remember the place you loved that felt safe and serene. It may have been a favorite vacation spot, a patch of grass under the spreading branches of a tree, a hideaway in the woods, a corner of the porch, a tree house, or even your own room. What was being in this place like for you? How did it soothe you? Transport yourself to this place in your mind. Sink into the calmness of the space. How did your little-girl heart feel in this place? Can you find this place of peace in your heart today? Where is the thread of you?

Ask your mother about her years as a young teen. What did she worry about more than anything? How did her anxiety affect her day-to-day behavior and choices? How was she able to stop the cycle of worry and find within herself God's place of peace?

What about her years as a little girl? When was she most at peace with herself? Did she have a special place that offered her a refuge from her worries? What was this place like? How does she access this place of peace in her heart today?

Candlelight Connection

When your story-sharing time has come to an end, place the candle in the corner between you and your mother. Become aware of the silence around you as you sit with the candle. Say this prayer together:

I'm worried, God.
My thread is full of knots.
They crowd into my heart
Until there's no room left for you.
I need some relief, God.
I need your help.
Help me to trust that all shall be well.
Remind me that worry
Blocks my path to you.
Open up my heart, God.
Loosen the knots that burden me.
Open up my heart, God,
To your gift of perfect peace.

Join hands with your mother and sit without speaking.
Nestle yourself into the silence that surrounds you. Feel God
loosen your knots of worry. Feel God's peace flow into your
heart and mingle with your mother's love. Feel God's peace
shine upon you and your mother like sunshine on a meadow.

When you are ready, blow out the candle, share a hug with
your mom, and go to sleep.

Chapter 3 *twists*

When People Are Mean to You

Looking Back

These stories come from Natalie, a mother who grew up in Illinois.

A Little Girl's Story

Melanie and I were best friends in fourth grade. One weekend, I spent hours at her house discussing the science reports that were due the next week. My topic was How Does Hair Grow? Our teacher, Mr. Jamison, required each of us to research our topic, write a report, and then give the report in front of the class.

I didn't like science, and I had no desire to dive into the research. Over the weekend, I confided my reluctance to Melanie. "I know all about hair!" Melanie said. "Just write down what I say." Only too happy to comply, I took notes while Melanie explained how hair grows. I soon had a page full of notes, plenty for a report. I took Melanie's word as the truth, and I was happy that my research was complete.

The day came for me to give my report. I shuffled to the front of the classroom and planted my feet close to the chalkboard. Looking out over the faces—in my small class there were all boys' faces except Melanie's—I caught Melanie's eye, and she gave me a reassuring smile. I cleared my throat and began to speak.

"New hairs grow from dead cells," I began, trying to keep my voice from shaking. "When the cells in your hair die, they come out of the little holes in your head," I continued, "and push out the new hairs."

"Stop," said Mr. Jamison. I looked at him, startled. His eyes bored holes through me. The back of my neck tingled. A feeling of dread spread over me like sticky syrup. "That's not correct, Natalie," Mr. Jamison said. "Where did you get your information?"

A hot flush crept into my cheeks. A throbbing began behind my eyes, and my heart hammered in my chest. "Uh . . . ," I stammered. Dots swirled before my eyes. My arms and legs turned to blocks of wood. What would I do now? I was in huge trouble. I couldn't tell Mr. Jamison that Melanie had told me what to write.

"Natalie, tell us where you got your information," said Mr. Jamison. His words pelted me like hailstones. My mind was blank. I couldn't think of anything to say.

A voice I recognized as Melanie's pierced the silence. "It's my fault, Mr. Jamison." All eyes turned to Melanie. "I told Natalie what to write," she said.

Mr. Jamison focused his stare at Melanie. "Your information is wrong, Melanie. You didn't research the topic. Next time you decide to help someone with a report, make sure you have your facts straight." As Mr. Jamison spoke, Melanie kept her gaze steady and held her head high. I stood frozen at the front of the classroom, stunned by what Melanie had done. She didn't have to take the blame for me. It would have been so easy for her not to say a word. Yet she spoke up for me, and I was grateful. Melanie had acted as a true friend.

Mr. Jamison didn't let me off the hook though. I still had to give a properly researched report about how hair grows. This time I got my information from a book. Through it all Melanie and I remained the best of friends.

A Young Teen's Story

One summer afternoon when I was thirteen, I opened our front door to Susan, my older sister's best friend. Susan and my sister Carol were high school freshmen. A year younger, I enjoyed their company, and we did many things together. We played for hours in our fenceless backyards. We rode bicycles, had water fights, sold lemonade, tossed the ball back and forth, and played hide-and-seek in the cornfields that bordered our backyards.

As I followed Carol out the door, Susan suggested we ride our bicycles to the neighborhood store to buy candy. I rushed back inside to get my money, then raced back out to the lawn to grab my bicycle. Already on their bicycles, Susan and Carol stared at me from the sidewalk. Susan's face twisted into a snarl. "'Bye, Natalie." She spoke in a mocking tone. "See you later."

Susan's words hit me like a torpedo and pushed all the air out of my lungs. My head wobbled. I couldn't speak. I gripped the handlebars of my bicycle, struggling to comprehend. A split second later, the impact of her meanness exploded in my heart: She didn't want me along! She had deliberately left me out. As I watched Carol and Susan pedal away, my face burned with humiliation. I let my bicycle drop to the grass. What had I done to make Susan hate me? I scoured my brain to remember the past few days. I must have done something to make her mad. I slumped away, the pain of Susan's sudden rejection stinging me like lemon juice in a fresh cut.

That September I started high school. One Saturday afternoon I sat on the stadium bleachers under the wide expanse of a crisp fall sky. Our football team had just scored a touchdown, and cheers erupted around me. I sprang up to clap and cheer too.

"Hey, Natalie!"

I turned around and saw Diane waving at me. I waved back, confused by her attention. I was a friend of Diane's, but not a good friend. Why was she suddenly interested in me? Diane snaked her way down to my row and squeezed in next to me. "Natalie," she said, "take a walk with me, would you?" She stood up, ready to go.

Why did Diane want to take a walk with me, especially in the middle of the football game? I glanced at the field, then back at Diane. "Oh, come on," she said. "Let's just go." I shrugged and followed her, wondering what was up.

We sauntered past the crowd and headed for the concession stand. Thinking that Diane wanted to buy a soda, I pulled out my money. Diane kept walking, though, and I stayed at her side. Within a few minutes, we had circled one side of the field and arrived at the stands reserved for the opposing team's supporters. A sprinkling of fans dotted the bleachers, and an anemic-sounding pep band struggled to play their school's fight song.

Without warning, Diane called to a tall boy who leaned against the bleachers. She flashed him a flirtatious smile, and with two quick strides, the boy, a sophomore, was at her side. They strolled together, and I plodded behind them, feeling like a tagalong little sister. Discomfort pricked at me. Why had I agreed to go on this walk? We hadn't gone far when the boy stopped, whirled around to face me, and blurted, "Would you beat it?"

Heat flooded into my cheeks. I turned and slinked away, the horrible truth socking me in the stomach: Diane had used me! She had used me so she could meet up with that guy and not be obvious about it. She didn't care about me at all. Why had she picked on me? What was it about me that invited her to use me like a pawn? I traced my steps back to our team's bleachers. I watched the rest of the game in silence, feeling like a crumpled candy wrapper.

Later that year I heard that Diane had dumped her boy-friend because he had come to school one morning with a bad haircut. This episode confirmed my sense of Diane as cruel and uncaring. I found some solace in knowing that I wasn't the only one who had suffered because of her actions.

As for Susan I never found out why she had so harshly excluded me. After that day we continued to spend hours together as part of the neighborhood group of kids, and nei-ther one of us ever mentioned the incident.

Finding the Thread

Have you ever received an unexpected gift of kindness? Did someone come forward to help you out of a tough situation? When Natalie was in fourth grade, her best friend Melanie admitted her role in an embarrassing fiasco when she could have easily remained silent. Natalie, amazed by her friend's unselfishness, recognized the act as a true kindness. She was grateful to Melanie, and their friendship continued for many years.

As she got older, Natalie experienced the flip side of kindness. When she was thirteen, her sister's friend Susan—out of the blue—excluded Natalie from a bicycle ride to the neighborhood store. Shocked and embarrassed, Natalie wondered what she had done to make Susan treat her that way and blamed herself for Susan's meanness.

At a high school football game, Diane, a so-called friend, talked Natalie into taking a walk with her. During the walk Diane "accidentally" ran into a boy she liked, and the boy turned on Natalie and told her to scram. Diane had used Natalie for her own selfish motive. Diane's heartlessness filled Natalie with an intense humiliation that lingered like the taste of raw onions. She wondered why Diane had picked her to carry out her scheme. She wondered what it was about her that invited Diane to see her as an easy target. Natalie's world darkened as doubts about herself filled her heart. The little girl she was—the fourth grader who had experienced a friend's kindness—cowered in the corner and refused to come out.

In time God's love softened the painful twists that gripped Natalie's heart. After Natalie learned Diane had dumped her boyfriend when he came to school with an unflattering haircut, Natalie's sense of Diane was confirmed: Diane was a person out of touch with the goodness in her heart, a person who used others only to satisfy her own whims. Natalie came to realize that Diane's cruel behavior had nothing to do with Natalie. She learned that Diane's actions said more about Diane than they did about her. Although Natalie never found out why Susan had been so cruel, she was able to accept God's gift of grace that offered her healing from the hurt. The little girl who had received her friend's act of kindness came alive. Natalie rediscovered her truth: She is worthy of true friendship and is cherished by a God whose love for her never diminishes. Today she is a woman of honesty and integrity, living a life that is open to the love of God.

Talk Time

What twists are in your thread right now? Has anyone been deliberately mean to you? Were you insulted, betrayed, hurt, or humiliated? How did you react? Has this person's actions confused you? Has the episode caused you to doubt yourself? Do you want to hide and never come out? Are you attempting to turn others against this person, or are you struggling to ignore the entire incident?

Settle in a quiet spot and think about your years as a little girl. Can you recall a time when someone was kind to you? Think about when a friend or adult offered a hug, a shoulder to cry on, a listening ear, helpful words, or an unexpected gift, and you felt special and loved as a result. Stay with the memory for a few moments. How did it feel to be on the receiving end of this kindness? Let yourself sink into the goodness that flowed from another's heart into yours. Can you recognize the little girl you were who knows the truth of herself? Can you find the little girl within you who can—in the face of meanness—hold on to her sense of herself? Where is the thread of you?

When you and your mother are comfortable ask your mother to recall a time as a young teen when someone was deliberately mean to her. How did she feel? What was her response? Did she keep the incident to herself or seek help? Was your mother able—by herself or with help—to keep herself centered despite the humiliation she felt? Now ask your mother about her little-girl years. Does she remember an occasion when someone was kind to her? What was it like for her? What message did the experience imprint on her heart? How did the experience of kindness help her cope during times when others were mean to her? In what ways does her little-girl heart continue to make a difference in her interactions with others?

Candlelight Connection

After your time of story sharing, place the candle in the corner between you and your mother. Give yourselves a few minutes to recognize that God is with you, as symbolized by the glowing flame. Say this prayer together:

> Someone was mean to me, God.
> Hateful words stormed into my heart
> And squeezed out the truth of me.
> Someone was mean to me, God.
> My thread is so twisted
> I feel like a pretzel.
> Show me your face, God.
> Yours is the true face of kindness.
> Soften the twists in my thread
> With the soothing balm of your love.
> Pour your love into my heart.
> Let your face shine through mine.
> Help me to reach for the truth,
> The truth that is me,
> The truth that leads me to you.

Reach for your mother's hands and hold them in yours. Remain silent for a few minutes. Feel God's love pour into your heart, softening all your painful twists. Feel God's love overflow from your heart and surge through your hands into your mother's hands. Feel the kindness of God blanket you and your mother in a soothing warmth.

When you are ready, blow out the candle, share a hug with your mom, and go to sleep.

Chapter 4 *loops*
When Life with Others Gets Complicated

Looking Back

These stories come from Zara, a mother who grew up in Ohio.

A Little Girl's Story

Seven girls came to my ninth birthday party that May. We played on the deck, laughing, talking, and tossing the Frisbee around. My next-door neighbor, Gail, flung the Frisbee into the air, but instead of reaching its intended target, it flew over the railing and landed down the steep cliff that bordered the back of our house. Before I could stop her, Gail was over the railing and climbing down the slope, shouting, "I'll get it!"

My older brother, my sister, and I would frequently climb down the cliff as a shortcut to a creek in Cuyahoga Valley National Recreation Area. Navigating past every root, plant, and dip on the incline required rock climbing ability, a skill that came as naturally to me as brushing my teeth. Gail had watched me climb down the cliff countless times, but had never tried it herself. Wondering how Gail would do, I scrambled to the edge of the deck to watch her. I could see her making steady progress down the cliff. Maybe she could do it after all.

When Gail was about five feet from the Frisbee, though, she froze. Her high-pitched wail filled the air. Motionless as a statue, she continued to cry. I realized she must have looked down and become frightened. Thoughts raced through my mind. My mother and another girl's mother were in the house. Should I go get them? Should we call the fire department?

At the same time, I realized that I was the only person around who was familiar with the shifting rocks and slippery clay-like soil. I had no doubt I could help Gail. Without waiting another second I scaled the railing and eased myself down the other side. My feet secured sure footing as I charted a path with my eyes and tested the route with my hands. In a minute I was at her side. I gently touched her arm, and Gail let out a choked whimper. Hooking her arm in mine, I tried to pull her toward me. Her trembling legs refused to budge.

"Come on, Gail, you have to move," I urged. "I've got you. Don't worry." I took a step, and Gail lurched toward me, her breathing shallow and fast. "You can do it," I said. "Take a deep breath and keep your eyes on me. Don't look down." Slowly, steadily, I guided Gail back up the cliff, pointing out where to place her feet and hands.

When Gail and I reached the railing, the other girls helped pull Gail, who was still shaking, to the deck. Gail wiped tears from her eyes and shuffled home, and we continued the party without her. After all the girls had gone home, I remembered that the Frisbee was still down the cliff.

A Young Teen's Story

The year I turned twelve, my whole life changed. One morning, without warning, my father left home. Leaving no note, he took only a few clothes and never showed up for his job as a construction contractor. I was not prepared for what happened to our family when he disappeared.

My mother didn't have a job at the time, and Father had just bought a new car that would have to be paid for. Besides that, workers had already dug a kidney-shaped hole in the backyard where our new swimming pool was to go. We had picked out the slide and the tile for the pool, and my brother, sister, and I could hardly wait for the project to be completed. Not only that, every kid in the neighborhood had their swimsuits ready in anticipation of their first plunge into our new pool.

We lived in a nice house and neighborhood with excellent schools, and Mom was determined to keep us in our home. She cut out every unnecessary frill. She halted construction on the pool. She took on three jobs so she could scrape together enough money to pay the mortgage. By day she worked as a secretary, rising at an early hour to clean office buildings before she was due at her desk. By night she worked as a waitress and didn't return home until late. Although I appreciated my mother's efforts, I hated that she didn't have time for me anymore.

Soon creditors began calling nonstop and showing up at the door, demanding payments we could no longer make. Tow trucks arrived to hitch up and haul away the new car and my father's construction equipment. For weeks the huge hole in our backyard blared out a billboard-sized reminder of our new status as a fatherless and poor family. One day workers came to fill in the hole. Our friends from the neighborhood watched the spectacle, disappointment etched on every face. Feeling as empty as the hole in the ground, I watched my dream pool turn into a big smoothed-over patch of dirt.

With my mother consumed by work, my brother, sister, and I were left to sort out our lives on our own. We did not mention my father. We never asked her, "Why did he leave?" or "How could this have happened?" When Mom was around she never brought up the subject, so neither did we. We followed the unspoken rule that drifted through our house like a floating marquee: *Don't talk about it.*

In the years before my father left, my parents had argued late at night more times than I could remember. My father had broken many promises, including a promise he made every year to build us a tree house. He had never been at home much. When he was around I sensed that he preferred my little sister to me, and I had clamored for his attention constantly. Although I knew the truth of family life with my father, I convinced myself that if my father would only return, everything would be fine.

In the wake of my father's disappearance, a barrage of emotions swept through our home. My normally upbeat brother sulked, talking in abrupt bursts only when necessary. My sister, eleven months younger than me, turned into a stranger. I had always had a close relationship with her, but now we argued all the time. We borrowed each other's clothes without asking and resorted to physical blows when enraged. No longer did we confide in each other. Our once pleasant conversations became vicious verbal assaults that stung me like a swarm of yellow jackets.

Three months after my father left, my grandfather, Papa, died. Over the years we had enjoyed long, intelligent conversations together about the past and the future. "You are smart," he had often told me. Many others saw him as an important person. That I had his attention made me feel special. When I once told him I wanted to be a veterinarian, he replied: "Don't waste your time on animals. Be a doctor and help humankind."

According to Papa, nothing was too hard or out of reach for me. His death tore another gaping hole in my already shredded family life.

Our dire financial situation made us eligible to receive food coupons. Ashamed that we needed to use them, Mom drove to the next town to buy groceries. One day as my sister and I unloaded the groceries from the car, Mom accidentally dropped a food coupon in the driveway. Busy carrying bags into the house, we didn't notice it. Later that afternoon, I saw Gail's older sister, Kim, pick up something from our driveway. I watched Kim with suspicion as she tucked the item in her pocket and scurried to her house next door. Kim had shown in the past that she had a mean streak. What did she have that belonged to us?

I found out the next day what it was that Kim had taken when her mother appeared at our door with an envelope. "Kim found this in your driveway," she said, handing me the envelope. I mumbled a quick "thank you" and shut the door. With shaking hands I tore open the envelope, fearing the worst. Inside was the dropped food coupon. Humiliation hit me like a sudden high fever. Kim knew! She knew we used food coupons! I didn't trust her with the information. For a long time, I lived in fear she would betray us by telling our friends.

Reading was my escape from the mess my family's life had become. I would grab a book and head outside—to the car in the driveway, a tree fort, a lean-to, or a hollow under the roots of a fallen tree. For hours at a time I read everything and anything from my grandmother's Harlequin romances to *National Geographic,* Philip Roth novels, and *Bury My Heart at Wounded Knee.* As I read Henri Charriere's *Papillon,* I gained a new appreciation for my life despite its difficulties.

Through books I not only escaped my reality, I learned things that I didn't learn in school, including hundreds of new words. My incessant reading and expanding vocabulary paid off with high scores on achievement tests at school. My father was gone, Papa had died, and life with my family would never be the same, but I had found a way to live with the changes.

My father did return for three months when I was eighteen years old. He stayed at his mother's house for a while and then got a job and an apartment in Cleveland. During a scheduled meeting with him, I was captivated by his charming smile and handsome face as he proudly showed my brother, sister, and me photographs of his work on a dam project in Arizona. He apologized, telling us he wanted to work things out with my mother.

My brother and sister refused to talk to Father. I struggled to find a middle ground between the anger and the hurt, but I soon realized that my father hadn't changed. I saw through the whitewash he painted on his sad and pathetic life to make it appear happy and productive. I couldn't ignore the feelings that welled up inside: I didn't like who my father was. I felt sorry for him. In the end my mother decided against a reconciliation, and my father disappeared again.

Finding the Thread

Have you ever wished you could go back to a simpler time of your life? a time when the lives of others didn't cause problems for you? As a nine-year-old, Zara knew exactly how to help her neighbor. When Gail panicked and froze on the spot, Zara didn't hesitate to rescue her. She was in control of the situation and used her physical agility and strength to guide her friend to safety. To Zara it was a simple matter to jump into action, a response that felt like the most natural thing in the world to her. Her neighbor was stuck on the cliff. She knew she could save her. What could be simpler than that?

The year Zara turned twelve her life became complicated. Her father left the family, leaving no clue to his whereabouts. Zara's mother took on three jobs to pay the mortgage, while her brother grew bitter and withdrew from the family. Zara and her sister began to squabble about everything. Nobody in the family talked about Father, whose sudden disappearance had thrust them into strange and bleak circumstances.

As her thread looped through the lives of her family, Zara struggled with relationships that had become painful, touchy, and hurtful. To add to the already challenging family situation, her revered grandfather died that same year, forcing Zara to endure yet another change. Life with her family had become as treacherous for Zara as a shortcut down a steep and slippery cliff.

During these years Zara found her escape in books. She combined her pleasure in reading with the simple joy of being outdoors. Reading about the trials and hardships of others helped her put her life into perspective. As an added benefit, she developed an extensive vocabulary and broader view of the world that brought her satisfaction and a sense of mastery.

Zara was once again like the nine-year-old who had kept her focus while rescuing her neighbor from the cliff. Teenaged Zara was able to retrieve her focus by losing herself in books. Reading nourished, enlightened, and sustained her. Through her reading, she was able to negotiate the constantly shifting terrain of her home life. Her thread still looped around the lives of her family, but she managed to stay on the path to God, the path that led her back to her heart.

Despite the complications of Zara's interpersonal relationships in her family, her sense of herself as someone strong, capable, and courageous returned. Today Zara is a woman who lets her heart be her guide. She engages fully in her life, offering comfort, joy, and strength to the lives that loop through hers.

Talk Time

Is your life crowded with the loops of parents, siblings, or friends? Are people complicating your life to the point that you wish they would leave you alone? Do you need room to think? Do you long for a simpler time, a time when you knew who you were in relation to others?

Remember yourself as a little girl. Was there a time when you didn't hesitate to act, when you knew without a doubt what your heart was telling you? a time when your heart was your undisputed guide along the path of your life? Drop into the memory for a few moments. What was it like to know yourself clearly within your heart even while living a life with others? Can you recognize that little-girl heart within yourself? Can you look in your heart and know that God is waiting to guide you through a life in relationship with others? Where is the thread of you?

After you and your mother have settled in your room, ask her about a time as a young teen when life with others caused her to be troubled, angry, or frustrated. How was her life made more complicated by friends, siblings, or parents? What did she do to restore a clear sense of herself? Now ask your mother to recall a time as a little girl when she was able to be herself and live a life of simple harmony with others. How does her little-girl heart reveal itself in her life today?

Candlelight Connection

After you and your mother have spent some time sharing stories, transfer the candle in the corner to a space between the two of you. Allow the candle's gentle light to bathe your room in the eternal love of God. Say this prayer together:

My thread loops through the lives of others, God.
Sometimes I wish it didn't.
Their lives cause me big problems,
And I want life to be simple again.
My heart gets cluttered
When everyone talks at once,
And I lose track of myself
When everyone changes so fast.
But you put other people in my world, God.
You want us to live for one another.
That's how I learn about me.
That's how I learn about you.
That's how I learn about love.
When life with others gets complicated,
Lead me through the loops, God.
Keep me on the path to you.
Reach for my hand in the darkness,
And walk with me along the way.

Join hands with your mother and remain silent for several
minutes. Feel God leading you through the loops in your
heart. Feel your hands enclosed in the hands of God. Feel God
in your mother's touch, guiding you, showing you the way. Feel
God wrap you and your mother in an everlasting embrace.

When you are ready, blow out the candle, share a hug with
your mom, and go to sleep.

Chapter 5 *Snags*
When You Lose Confidence

Looking Back

These stories come from Simone, a mother who grew up in Oregon.

A Little Girl's Story

When *Mary Poppins* hit the movie theaters the year I turned nine, my enthusiasm for singing reached a crescendo. After seeing the movie, I listened to the *Mary Poppins* soundtrack over and over, memorizing all the lyrics and singing along. Music was my whole world. My mother often told me I could carry a tune before I learned to talk. I had also been figuring out songs on the piano from an early age and taking piano lessons since I was five. It wasn't long before I was playing the *Mary Poppins* songs by ear. "Chim Chim Cher-ee," sung by Bert the chimney sweep, was my favorite song from the movie. As I polished the song on the piano, I got a wonderful idea. Why not create a song-and-dance act for our school's annual talent show?

I pitched the idea to four friends. They responded enthusiastically, and we plunged into the project.

Fueled by my determination to win first place in the talent show, I poured all my energy into making the act the best anyone had ever seen. I practiced with my friends every day after school. I taught them to sing "Chim Chim Cher-ee" while I accompanied them on the piano. One girl helped choreograph a chimney sweep dance routine, but there was no doubt I was the group's musical leader. By the time it was our turn to perform on the big night, I had made sure we were ready. The fourth-grade chimney sweeps filed onstage, charcoal smeared on their faces, wearing black costumes and carrying charcoal-blackened brooms. Also wearing black—dress, tights, and shoes—I struck the first note on the piano, and the chimney sweeps kicked in unison. My fingers flew over the keys, and I sang along with the dancers, losing myself in the familiar lyrics, the melody, and the hot stage lights.

When the last note resounded on the piano, the auditorium fell silent, but only for a second. Then applause burst out, long and loud. As whistles and cheers erupted from the audience, I felt like I was floating. At the end of the talent show, our group was awarded first prize. We had done it! Nothing could stop me now!

A Young Teen's Story

I hated my sixth-grade teacher. I thought Mrs. Malone was crabby, strict, and about as much fun as getting a shot at the doctor's office. Although I had always been a well-behaved student, I set out to annoy her.

One day I was alone in the classroom with my friend Ricky when I thought of the perfect way to torture the teacher. That year, a cinnamon-toothpick fad had swept our school. Like many kids, Ricky carried a vial of cinnamon oil and a supply of toothpicks for dipping into the oil and giving to friends to suck on. Knowing Mrs. Malone was allergic to cinnamon, I convinced Ricky to pour the contents of his vial onto her desk. Within seconds the potent scent of cinnamon filled the air. We scuttled out the door to avoid detection and came back inside a few minutes later with the rest of the students.

The effect was immediate. When Mrs. Malone sat at her desk, her face reddened and she began sneezing. Tears gushed from her eyes, and between sneezes she wheezed. Another boy knew Ricky had a vial of cinnamon oil and guessed what Ricky had done. Word spread through the classroom and got back to Mrs. Malone. She confronted Ricky, then sent him to the principal's office. Moments later she followed Ricky out the door, wiping her streaming eyes with a handkerchief.

While the room buzzed with chatter, I sat silently at my desk. Minutes ticked by. What was Ricky telling the principal? He wouldn't give me away, would he? The door opened and I jumped. The custodian, sponge and bucket in hand, marched to Mrs. Malone's desk and scrubbed its surface. I wrestled with more questions. What would I do if Ricky told on me? I could never admit to doing such a thing. I had never been in trouble before. I wouldn't get in trouble now, would I?

The door rattled open. Heart pounding in my chest, I watched the school secretary poke her head in. She looked right at me. "Simone," she said, her voice sharp as a needle, "come with me, please." An intense heat prickled my head and spread to my cheeks. Feeling like a rag doll, I stumbled to the door, while a flurry of whispers whipped through the classroom.

Seated with Ricky before the principal, I put on my most innocent expression. "I didn't have anything to do with it!" I declared when the principal asked me to explain myself. I refused to admit my part in the caper, insisting that it was all

Ricky's idea. Ricky followed me from the office, and when we reached the hallway, he began to cry. Trembling all over, I whispered to Ricky: "I'm so sorry. I was afraid of getting into trouble."

Ricky wiped his eyes with the backs of his hands. Staring at the floor, he said, "I understand." Ricky's empathy touched me, but not enough to stop me from hatching other devious plots.

My eighth-grade French teacher was an elderly woman who wore a hearing aid. One day I thought of a great way to entertain the class. When the teacher asked the class a question, I raised my hand. She called on me, but, instead of speaking out loud, I mouthed the answer.

"What?" she asked in French, fiddling with her hearing aid. Knowing she was turning up the volume, I mouthed the answer again. The teacher started down the aisle toward me, all the while adjusting her hearing aid. Twice more I mouthed the words. When she was right next to me, I blasted her, shouting out the answer as loud as I could. She jumped back and collided with the next row of desks, nearly falling down. My classmates roared with laughter, and I laughed along with them. The teacher sent a report home to my parents. My mother insisted that I apologize, which I did eventually, but I could tell from the look on my teacher's face that she knew I wasn't sincere.

That same year I had a serious crush on Wayne, a notorious "bad boy." Desperate to attract his attention, I decided I had to do something bad to get him to notice me. My English teacher walked with a limp. One day she asked me to help her pass out papers to the class. Here was my chance! I followed her up and down the rows, imitating her crooked gait. Muffled snickers filled the classroom, and a quick glance at Wayne told me he had not only noticed but was impressed. The teacher didn't catch me that time, but after several weeks she sent a report to my parents stating that I was spending too much time talking with Wayne.

Not wanting to get into trouble anymore, I decided to calm down for the remainder of the year. I graduated from junior high school without any further classroom incidents. However, the summer before I began ninth grade, my life changed considerably.

My mother noticed that the hemlines of all my dresses hung unevenly around my legs. On closer inspection, she discovered that one of my shoulders was higher than the other one and my hip stuck out at an odd angle. She took me to the doctor, who diagnosed me with a curvature of the spine called scoliosis. His solution was to put me in a full-body cast and subject me to bed rest for nine months, and then for me to have spinal fusion surgery if my spine started to curve again. Outraged, I cried for hours, telling my mother I would never consent to missing a whole year of school.

A second doctor suggested a different treatment—a back brace. After much consideration my family decided this was the better option for me. Thinking only that I had escaped the dreaded body cast, I agreed to wear the brace. I soon discovered that maybe the brace was an even worse fate.

The brace reached down to my hips and hugged me like a girdle. A long metal bar protruded from the top of my clothes and ended in a shelf for my chin. Two more padded metal bars supported the back of my head. It was as if my head was in a cage. In my bizarre metal contraption, visible for all to see, I felt like a walking carnival freak show.

I had to wear the brace all the time for two years. In ninth grade, the last year of junior high, at least I had friends who had known me before I got the brace. When I entered high school the next year, however, I didn't know a lot of the kids. Feeling the stares and hearing the whispers as I stepped into my classrooms was more than I could bear. I dreaded the open-jawed looks and stifled laughs that confronted me daily as I walked the hallways. To protect myself from ridicule, I tried to avoid new situations, and I spent as much time as I could by myself.

One friend refused to let me shut her out of my life. Trying to be supportive and kind, she offered me words of advice. "Just be yourself," she said. "Do what everybody else does. You don't want to be known as 'the girl in the brace.'" I tried to follow her suggestions, but I felt awkward at first. How could I do what everybody else does? I was exempt from gym class, couldn't participate in a sport, and didn't have the nerve to attend the school dances.

I liked math and music, though, so I started there. I put forth my best effort in math class and made great strides in my studies. I continued my piano lessons and performed with a choral group, brace and all. Participating in these activities gave me a deep sense of satisfaction and pleasure. Slowly I came out of my shell.

Finding the Thread

Have you ever lost confidence in yourself, causing your thread to hit a snag? Did you find yourself scrambling to recover your lost sense of yourself in any way you could? Perhaps you gave up instead, convinced you would never be able to feel good about yourself again. At age nine Simone wowed the audience at the school talent show with her flawless performance at the piano and clever direction of the song and dance act. As she entered adolescence, however, something changed. She began funneling her energy and talent into misbehavior.

Simone had never before caused trouble in class, but in sixth grade she wanted to annoy her teacher simply because Simone didn't like her. Aware that her teacher was allergic to cinnamon, Simone convinced Ricky to pour cinnamon oil on the teacher's desk. By refusing to admit her role in the scheme, Simone forced her friend to take all the blame.

In junior high, Simone's mischief escalated as she focused her efforts on entertaining the class and impressing a "bad" boy. She knew her behavior was hurtful, but the look of admiration in her classmates' eyes as they witnessed her antics was too enticing to give up. Poking fun at the physical limitations of her teachers gave Simone the attention she craved.

The summer after eighth grade, Simone was diagnosed with scoliosis. Forced to wear a corrective back brace, she found herself on the receiving end of whispers and stares, and she retreated within herself. The little girl she used to be—the nine-year-old girl who had directed a prizewinning song and dance act—was nowhere to be found.

With the help of a friend who saw beyond her brace to the real girl inside, Simone was able to remember who she was. When she made a conscious effort to use her God-given talents in a positive way, her confidence gradually returned. Today Simone is a woman who uses her musical gifts to bring joy to herself and to others.

Talk Time

Is your confidence in yourself at a low point? What happened that has caused your thread to hit a snag? Have you lost track of the real you? Are you searching for ways to feel better about yourself, perhaps even self-destructive, dangerous, or cruel ways, that boost your image in the eyes of others? Have you hidden yourself away, refusing to try anymore?

What do you remember about your years as a little girl? Think about a time when you had all the confidence in the world, a time when you knew you could do anything you tried. Stay with the memory for a few minutes. How does it feel to relive this experience? Can you recognize this little girl in your life today? Where is the thread of you?

Your mother likely has memories of a time when she was your age and was losing confidence in herself. As you settle in your candlelit bedroom with your mother, ask her to tell you about an occasion as a young teen when she no longer believed in herself. What happened? How did she feel about herself? What did she do to cope with the situation? What did she do to get her confidence back?

Now ask your mother about her years as a little girl. What story comes to her mind? What memory does she have of herself that speaks boldly of her confidence and courage? Where is that confident little girl in her heart today? How does that little girl show herself in your mother's life today?

Candlelight Connection

After you and your mom have shared your stories, bring the candle in the corner to a space between the two of you. Spend a few moments in silence, watching the light that signals God's presence with you. Say this prayer together:

My thread has hit a snag, God.
My confidence is gone.
I'm just an ordinary kid.
I have nothing special to offer.
But you are here, God,
Telling me I am unique and precious,
Reminding me of my talents,
The talents that live in my heart.
You gently tug at my snag, God.
You get me unstuck from its snarls.
You help me remember
Who I am meant to be.

Now hold hands with your mother. Sit in silence for a few minutes. Notice God in the quiet that surrounds you. Feel God at work in your heart, gently tugging at your snag. Feel God's healing touch in the touch of your mother's hands. Feel God's warmth and love pulsate through your hands into the very core of your being.

When you are ready, blow out the candle, share a hug with your mom, and go to sleep.

Chapter 6 *coils*
When You Are Confused

Looking Back

These stories come from Hedda, a mother who grew up in southwestern Germany.

A Little Girl's Story

My two-year-old brother stood at the casket, which sat in the middle of our living room. My father lay inside, a scar creasing his cheek. My brother stared at my father and said, "You should climb out of that box." My father had been in a fatal car accident. I wasn't quite five years old, and like my brother, I was puzzled. Why didn't my father just get up?

One of my mother's relatives was a seamstress, and for the funeral she had sewn identical black-and-white check suits for my sisters and me. On the day of the funeral I put on my new suit, white stockings, and black shoes. The short jacket had a round collar and big black buttons down the front. The skirt had two little pleats at the waist and a generous cut so it flared in a wide circle when I twirled. The fabric had a rich texture that I loved to smooth with my hands.

At the funeral my mother's face crumpled and glistened with tears as relatives and friends hugged her. I knew I was supposed to be sad too. How could I be sad, though, when I was wearing the most beautiful suit in the world? Grown-ups approached my two older sisters, my brother, and me, saying, "You poor children." I didn't understand what they meant. Why were we poor children? Running the luxurious folds of my skirt between my fingers, I felt anything but poor. Still a sliver of shame nagged at me. I knew I shouldn't have been enjoying my new clothes. I knew my father's death was the reason I had been given such a fine garment.

After the funeral my mother, who had always been an industrious knitter, increased her output. I heard her footsteps in the middle of the night and knew she was awake, working on her knitting projects. Socks, sweaters, hats, scarves, and mittens flew off her needles. During the day I sat with her as she knitted, enjoying the satisfying click-click of the needles and the soothing sound of the radio. Although I loved to play outdoors I became fascinated with watching her knit.

My mother soon taught me how to knit and crochet. I was a quick learner. My grandmother was a frequent visitor, and together the three of us knitted as we sat by the radio. Whenever I got restless I took my knitting outside and worked my needles as gentle breezes ruffled my hair. By the time I was in elementary school, I could knit socks using five needles.

When I was about eight years old, I began to crochet clothes for my doll. I made dresses, pants, and skirts for her. My second cousins saw what I was doing and clamored for hand-crocheted clothes for their own dolls. I took their orders and worked steadily, whipping out the clothes so fast my cousins were amazed. My aunt and uncle marveled at my cleverness and speed. I beamed with pride at their praise.

Not only did I crochet for my cousins, I used my skills at school. *Handarbeit,* which means "handwork," was part of the curriculum in German schools. Our teacher, Frau Braun, taught us knitting and crocheting, and I was the star of the fourth-grade class. At the end of fourth grade Frau Braun started us on something new—crocheting a white baby jacket and hat. This was a complex project, but my teacher saw that I would be able to do it. When I changed schools for the fifth grade and was no longer in Frau Braun's class, she invited me to her home to finish the baby clothes. Spending time with my teacher in her home, working with my hands to create beautiful things, was a special honor. I decided then that I would become a teacher of *handarbeit,* just like Frau Braun.

A Young Teen's Story

The phone rang in the middle of the night and jangled me awake. I heard my mother answer and speak in hushed tones. When she hung up, my older sister, younger brother, and I huddled around her. "Your sister has been in a car accident," Mother told us. "I'm going to the hospital."

Every Friday night my two sisters, ages fifteen and seventeen, went to a sports activity club close to home. They always went together and had fun socializing with friends. That night, after attending the club, my oldest sister got in a car with a group of friends. My other sister did not, choosing instead to head home. Now my oldest sister was in the hospital.

Horror flashed through my mind. Would my sister's accident prevent me from going to an upcoming birthday party, a party I had looked forward to for weeks? I couldn't bear to think of everyone but me having fun at the party. Already I had planned what I would wear to this party. The next moment, guilt engulfed me like a tidal wave. How could I even think about going to a party at a time like this? My sister could be seriously injured. Yet I had to admit to myself that I didn't want to miss the party for anything.

A neighbor took care of us while Mother was gone. "Your sister will be fine," our neighbor said. I clung to her words with my whole heart, repeating them to myself over and over. Yes, my sister would be fine and would come home. I was relieved to think that my life soon would return to normal.

My mother came home in the morning to change her clothes, then left for the hospital again. My sister, brother, and I walked together to school. That afternoon we all went to the hospital to visit our oldest sister. I was shocked at her bruised and swollen face. Scary looking stitches marked her cheeks and chin, and she looked small and pale against the pillow. Her eyes fluttered open and settled on my face. I managed to smile at her, all the while believing she would be fine.

A week later, with my sister still in the hospital, I took the city train to the long-awaited birthday party. I wore a pretty green skirt, a favorite brown sweater, and a custom-made set of black and gold chains. For the duration of the party I refused to feel guilty about having fun while my sister lay in a hospital bed. I had a wonderful time with my friends.

The next Sunday—my sister's tenth day in the hospital— my mother got a phone call. As she listened the color drained from her face, and I knew something was terribly wrong. She herded my other sister and me into the car and drove as fast as she could to the hospital. By the time we got there my sister had already died from a blood clot.

Mother fell apart. She collapsed against the nurse and screamed. My sister backed against a wall and slid down to her knees, her eyes empty and glazed. I watched them both, unable to move. The nurse turned to me. "Can you drive them home?" she asked.

I blinked. The legal driving age in Germany was eighteen. I was only thirteen. Did I look old enough to drive? Did I look like I had everything under control? How could I be so calm? Was I not fazed by my sister's death? What was wrong with me? Confusion swirled through my head.

Besides feeling confused I felt betrayed when my sister died. I had believed my sister would be fine, and I had not realized the severity of her injuries. I had gone to the party when my sister had been close to death. Our neighbor had not told me the truth when she said my sister would be fine.

After my sister's funeral, my mother retreated into her own world, unable to look beyond her own pain. My surviving sister withdrew as well, quitting the sports activity club, refusing to see friends, barricading herself in her room. I knew the heavy burden she carried. She thought she should have prevented our sister from getting into that car. I carried my own burden, and a million questions plagued me. Why hadn't I seen the truth for myself? Why had I believed the neighbor? There seemed to be no answers to the questions that haunted me.

Our family was obligated by tradition to observe a year-long period of mourning by wearing dark clothing. My sister and I wore black, high-necked dresses every day, often with black silky scarves. My sister had died December 1, and as the Christmas season approached, I longed to wear colorful clothes. I wanted to feel happy again. Mother encouraged my sister and me to quit wearing black. "You're just children," she said. "You can wear other colors now." I didn't feel right about that though. Wearing different colors brought joy into my life, and I thought I shouldn't feel joy. I thought that if I felt bad I shouldn't look good.

Several weeks after the funeral the tears, silence, and sadness that permeated our home were more than I could bear. I escaped to the outside world and spent time with my friends, immersing myself in fun and laughter. But whenever I returned home to my grieving mother and sister, my confusion returned. Why didn't I feel sad like they did? What was wrong with me?

The next year I took dance classes at school and joined a club that held Sunday afternoon dances. Since my sister's death, I had not spent a lot of time knitting and crocheting. I decided to crochet a dress I could wear to the dances. I worked on it for days, using a pattern for a fitted bodice and long sleeves and correcting mistakes so they didn't show. The dress had a blue background and an array of colors that came together in a vibrant triangle at the front of its long flowing skirt. When I wore my new rainbow dress I came alive.

Finding the Thread

Have you ever been confused by your reactions to a life event? Have you ever thought you should feel the way everybody else does about something? Have questions filled your heart, questions to which you had no answers?

When Hedda was very young she suffered a profound personal loss—the sudden death of her father. Entranced by beautiful clothes, she delighted in the brand-new suit she was given to wear for her father's funeral, even though she knew she was supposed to be feeling sad. Although her behavior may have seemed inappropriate, she had found her own way to cope with the grief that surrounded her.

In the weeks following Hedda's father's death the little girl became enthralled with the knitting that kept her mother busy. Hedda discovered within herself a natural talent for handwork. The thrill of creating her own beautiful, colorful garments also helped her to live with the loss of her father.

Tragedy struck again during Hedda's thirteenth year. Her seventeen-year-old sister died of injuries she suffered in a car accident. The death caused Hedda's world to collapse. The young teen's thread coiled with confusion as she endlessly questioned herself about her behavior in the days before and after her sister's death. Hedda wondered why she had allowed herself to believe that her sister would recover. She wondered how she could stay so calm in the face of such a tragedy. She wondered why she didn't cry as her mother and surviving sister did.

For weeks the tears of Hedda's mother and sister flooded their home. The atmosphere of sorrow began to chafe at Hedda until she was no longer able to stand the sadness. She sought solace with her friends, yet her confusion and guilt lingered.

Slowly a sense of joy returned to Hedda's life. Amid the questions that had no answers Hedda unearthed her love of handwork and crocheted a colorful dress she could wear with pride. The work brought her healing. The lively five-year-old who twirled around in her new funeral suit, the eight-year-old who crocheted doll clothes for her cousins, and the fourth-grader who was the star knitter of the class all came alive within her heart and burst through the coils of confusion. When she rediscovered her love of handwork, she rediscovered herself.

God lives in Hedda today. She is a woman with a clear sense of style, a woman who loves to surround herself with color and texture, a woman who lives with questions that may never have any answers. Her little-girl heart shows her the way.

Talk Time

Is your thread coiled in confusion? Are you happy one minute and sad the next? Angry one minute and afraid the next? Is your heart filled with questions that do not have answers? Are you crying, but you do not know why? Are you dry-eyed when you think you should be crying? Are you so confused you don't know what you are feeling? Confusion can hit at any time, for any reason, and the coils in your thread can make it hard to remember who you are.

What do you recall from your years as a little girl? Was there a time when you knew without a doubt that joy lived within you? a time when your life was like a cobalt-blue autumn sky, clear and crisp as far as you could see? a time you felt strong, secure, and steady? a time you knew that nothing could come between you and your natural sense of playfulness, belonging, and purpose? Close your eyes and ponder the memories that float to the surface. Are you able to find your little-girl heart? Where is the thread of you?

When you and your mother have gathered in your candlelit space, ask her to tell you a story from her early teen years. Invite her to share about a time when she was confused, when her emotions jarred her, when she did not understand why she was feeling as she did. What was the experience like for her? Was there anybody she turned to for help?

Next ask your mom to tell you stories about herself as a little girl. When did she have the clearest picture of who she really was? What gave her joy? How does that little girl show herself in her life today?

Candlelight Connection

After you and your mother have shared your stories, transfer the candle in the corner to a space between the two of you. Spend a few moments watching the flame and listening to the silence around you. Say this prayer together:

I'm caught in the coils, God,
The coils of confusion.
I'm one big jumble inside,
And nothing makes sense.
I cry and I don't know why.
I don't cry and I wonder why.
I'm filled with questions,
And I don't have any answers.
But I do know this:
When I cry and I don't know why,
You kiss my tears and I know you understand.
When my eyes stay dry and I'm mixed up inside,
You hold me in your arms and I feel safe and loved.
In the mystery that is my life,
Lead me to my heart, God.
Through the coils, I can always find you there.

Join hands with your mother and share a few quiet moments together. Let yourself sink gently into the silence. Know that God is hidden among the coils of your heart, comforting and caressing you. Feel God in your mother's hands, a whirl of blues, yellows, and reds. Feel God encircle you and your mother with a rainbow of tenderness.

When you are ready, blow out the candle, share a hug with your mom, and go to sleep.

Chapter 7 *spirals*
When Your Life Feels Out of Control

Looking Back

These stories come from Patricia, a mother who grew up in New York.

A Little Girl's Story

Saturdays meant subway rides. My mother and I left the dangerous neighborhood we lived in and rode to her place of work, to the beach, or to Grandmother's house—a ninety-minute ride away. My imaginary friend, a twelve-inch-high elf named Little Robin, rode with me, perched as always on my shoulder. Little Robin was magical, and I thought I was a little magical too. One Saturday when I was five Little Robin and I boarded the subway with my mother so we could visit Grandmother. Bouncing into a seat, I studied the people who sat around me.

Every one of the adults I saw looked grouchy. Their mouths turned down at the corners, their eyes held fierce stares, and their shoulders slumped as if they were burdened with invisible loads. Why were they all so unhappy? As I looked around, I thought of a fun way to amuse myself during the long ride: I would pick out the crankiest looking grown-ups and smile at them until they smiled back.

From my seat next to my mother, I could see a long lineup of scowling adults, each person just begging for a smile. My eyes settled on a large man bundled in a shabby coat and wearing slacks crisscrossed with wrinkles. A deep frown creased his forehead, and he glared at me. I decided he would be the subject of my first experiment. Tossing my head so my pigtails brushed my shoulder, I flashed him a wide smile.

The frowning man continued to glare at me. I smiled like I had never smiled before, determined to make him smile back at me. Seconds passed, then a minute. I didn't give up. With Little Robin on my shoulder cheering me on, I knew I could crack through his frown.

I noticed the difference in the man's eyes first. They changed from cold marbles to pools of light. Slowly his mouth curled upward and joined his eyes in a twinkling smile. My own eyes danced with joy. It worked! I had made him smile. One by one I smiled at every cranky grown-up I could find, coaxing a smile from each unhappy face.

I never got tired of my new game. From that day on I played it every time I rode the subway, always savoring the thrill of changing frowns into smiles. It was my way of sprinkling a little magic on the world.

A Young Teen's Story

From the time I entered first grade I had trouble concentrating on my schoolwork. My family and I lived in a housing project, where the neighborhood was so dangerous my two brothers and I were not allowed to play outside. Inside I lived with a lot of yelling, fighting, and dish throwing. I never knew when my alcoholic father would fly into a rage and come after me with the strap. My mother tried to provide a decent home life for us, but we lived in almost constant chaos.

As a second grader I wished for some information, anything that would help me survive life at home. The subjects I studied at school—addition, subtraction, reading, and writing—did not give me the information I needed. I had no inkling that as bad as the situation was then, it would only get worse as I grew older.

When I was twelve my parents put my sixteen-year-old brother in charge of caring for my other brother and me while our parents worked. From the start the arrangement was barely tolerable. My oldest brother insisted that I ask permission to read a book, eat a snack, or even go to the bathroom. He carved out a niche for himself as a dictator who controlled my every move.

Soon my life spiraled out of control. My brother began to sexually abuse me. He chased me around the house, cornered me, and forced me to do unimaginable things. Day after nightmarish day he came after me. If I didn't comply with his demands, he made my life even more miserable.

One day I spent hours hiding from my brother. I managed to stay just out of his reach, a tactic that enraged him. When my father got home from work, my brother launched into a tirade, telling Father how I had refused to obey him. He made it sound like I was an uncooperative brat. Of course my brother didn't tell my father that it was his sexual advances that I had refused. Nor did I.

A tornado blew through my head. My brother was the one in the wrong, not me. Fury burned in me like red-hot coals, but I didn't have time to let my anger rise to the surface.

Watching my father closely, I could see he had arrived home already agitated and in a volatile mood. Without warning he grabbed me and began to strike me with the strap. As I endured the cruel punishment, I could see my brother smirking at me. I longed to tell Father the truth about my brother. That would wipe that smirk off his face once and for all.

In Father's holster, only inches away from my face when I was being beaten, was Father's gun. It was the gun he carried for his job as a bridge and tunnel officer. As soon as I saw the gun I knew I was doomed to suffer again and again at the hands of my brother. I realized I would never be able to tell Father the truth about what my brother was doing to me. If I did I was sure Father would whip out that gun and shoot my brother. I didn't want to have that on my conscience.

Telling my mother what was going on was out of the question as well. She was overwhelmed with her full-time job, with paying the bills, and with trying to keep our home running, even at a barely functional level. I thought that if I told her she might have an emotional breakdown and be sent away. Where would that leave me? I would be left at home with my abusive brother and my unpredictable father. No, I couldn't tell my mother.

I was also afraid to tell my schoolteacher what was happening at home. I did not want to be responsible for my father's actions if he should find out what my brother was doing to me. I struggled to concentrate on multiplication, long division, fractions, reading, government, and history. None of these things held any relevance for me. Afraid to reveal my secret, I was caught in a hideous trap with no way to escape.

When I entered eighth grade I realized I could create my own sphere of happiness away from my brother and father. Although my life at home was unbearable, life at school didn't have to be. So I started to smile at my classmates, friends, and teachers. At first I had to force myself to do it. Many times I felt as parched and cracked as a sunbaked desert. I thought if I kept smiling, my face might break into a million pieces. Still I smiled even when I didn't feel like it.

After a while my face changed. My muscles seemed less rigid. My mouth began to naturally turn up at the corners. I felt a light shine through my eyes, a light that poured forth from my heart. I smiled so much that my English teacher, a severe and stern nun, called me Miss Sunshine. I loved my honorary title and wore it proudly, trying to smile whenever I could.

My smiling changed nothing at home though. The abuse continued until I got the courage to move out at age sixteen. Once gone from the house, I confided in a trustworthy person who was willing to help me reveal my secret. With my friend's encouragement, I gained the confidence to confront my brother. I told my brother that if he continued to abuse me, my friend would tell our parents or go to the authorities. After that conversation my brother stopped abusing me. Until that time I had done what I could to make my life bearable.

Finding the Thread

Have you ever been in an unbearable situation you felt helpless to change? Have you experienced something so terrible and overwhelming that it eclipsed everything else, something so big that it threatened the very thread of your being?

Patricia describes the anguish she suffered as a child and young teen in a chaotic household in which eventually she was a victim of sexual abuse. From an early age she was locked in a fierce battle for the mere survival of her spirit.

Through sheer strength of will, her spirit did survive. As a five-year-old Patricia discovered a way to get grouchy subway riders to smile. Her life at home was a mess, but she found, even at that young age, that she could plant the seeds for happiness in herself and others with a simple yet powerful action: smiling.

At age twelve Patricia's life spiraled out of control. Desperate and alone, she searched for a shred of hope in her bleak existence and found it deep within herself—in her little-girl heart. Patricia began to smile again—not because her life was wonderful but because in some way she must have felt a connection with God and the thread of her being. The little girl who had smiled at grown-ups on the subway had been there all along, and she called up that little-girl spirit to help her through an almost unbearable chapter of her life.

Despite the misery Patricia had to endure, her heart lay safe among the spirals. She knew in her heart that she had what it takes to lead a happy life. The scared, lonely girl Patricia once was grew up to become the strong woman she is today—a woman steeped in love and gratitude.

Talk Time

Is your life out of control? Do you feel yourself spiraling higher and higher, caught in a situation that has you feeling you are about to fall from a tightrope with no safety net below you? Are you unsure of what to do? Are you frightened and feeling alone? Do you wish you had somebody to turn to?

Think about your experiences as a little girl. Was there a moment when you knew that you had the power within you—in the face of crisis—to emerge with your spirit intact and thriving? What did you do? How did you discover that your heart was strong and wise and would carry you through? Let the memory wash over you for a few minutes. Can you recognize your little-girl heart in your life now? Where is the thread of you?

After you and your mom light your candle in the corner, review the "Quick Safety Guide" found in "Getting Started." Then ask your mom if she ever experienced a situation as a young teen that sent her life spiraling out of control. Invite her to tell you about it, but understand that it may be hard for her to share with you. What was it like for her? Was she able to call upon her little-girl heart for help? How did that help her cope with the experience?

Now ask your mother about her years as a little girl. What stories does she recall that speak of her strength and courage in the face of hardship? Where in her life today does she continue to cherish and celebrate her little-girl heart?

Candlelight Connection

After you and your mother have shared your stories, take the candle from the corner and set it between the two of you. Take time to bask in the flickering flame. Recognize that its light represents God's abiding presence with you. Say this prayer together:

My thread is spiraling, God.
Higher and higher I go.
It's lonely up here, God, and I'm so afraid of falling.
Remind me that you are with me.
Remind me that you live in my heart.
Help me to listen to your voice within me,
Your voice that helps me remember
That you cradle me with tenderness
That you have loved me forever
That you and I are one
And you will never leave me.
My life is hard, God.
I wish it were easier.
But if life has to be hard, then send me what I need.
Your grace flows through my spirals,
Surrounding me with light, peace, and hope.
And I know
You will catch me if I fall.

Reach for your mother's hands. Because God speaks most clearly to us in the quiet moments, spend a few minutes in silence. Listen for God's voice within your heart. Feel it spill forth in a cascade that washes over you, spirals and all. Feel God's voice flood through your fingertips as you sit, hands joined with your mother's. Feel God's voice bathe you and your mom in comforting light.

When you are ready, blow out the candle, share a hug with your mom, and go to sleep.

Your Personal Reflections

I am interested in hearing from you, special reader. What did you especially like about this book? Which chapter(s) resonated most strongly with you? What have you learned about yourself? Do you see your life in a different way as a result of reading this book? Do you see your life as a constant thread of stories? What was most helpful?

What was it like to read this book and share it with your mother? How did you like the experience of creating sacred space with her? What was it like to tell your mother your stories and hear some of her stories? What have you learned about your mother? How has your relationship with her changed since you experienced the sharing that this book suggests? Have you grown closer to each other?

What have you learned about God and your relationship with God? Has your relationship with God deepened in any way? Have you grown closer to God?

I would love to hear what you have to say. When you visit my Web site, *www.eileenpettycrew.com,* you'll have the opportunity to post your comments, stories, and suggestions anonymously and see what other readers have to say, too. (Your mom may want to post her comments as well.)

Thank you.

Eileen Pettycrew

Closing Prayer

God everywhere, God with me, God in my heart,
Guide me as I grow.
In the middle of chaos,
Keep me safe.
In the middle of heartache,
Keep me close to you.
When my world feels crazy,
And I lose track of who I am,
Lead me to my true self.
Help me remember that you and I are one,
Together in love,
Together in joy,
Together in peace
For all eternity.